RAINBOW

D0643983

6.C
.5

GYMNASTICS

Junior Sports

Morgan Hughes

Rourke
Publishing LLC
Vero Beach, Florida 32964

www.rourkepublishing.com

PHOTO CREDITS: Cover, p 13, 21, 29 Stephen Dunn/Getty; title page, p 5, 12 Brian
Bahr/Getty; p 6 Photos.com; p 9 Timothy Clary/Getty; p 11 Gary Prior/Getty; p 15
Darren McCollester, Getty; p 17 Ruth Gray/Getty; p 18 Doug Pensinger/Getty; p 22,
26, 27, 28 Iko Lee, Getty; p 23 Hector Mata/Getty; p 25 John Dominis/Getty

Title page: *Few athletic disciplines combine physical strength, endurance, and artistry the
way gymnastics do.*

Editor: Frank Sloan

Library of Congress Cataloging-in-Publication Data

Hughes, Morgan, 1957-
  Gymnastics / Morgan Hughes.
      p. cm. -- (Junior sports)
  Includes bibliographical references and index.
  ISBN 1-59515-191-5 (hardcover)
  1. Gymnastics--Juvenile literature. I. Title. II. Hughes, Morgan, 1957- Junior sports.
  GV461.3.H85 2004
  796.4'4--dc22
                                    2004009371

Printed in the USA

CG/CG

TABLE OF CONTENTS

WHY GYMNASTICS?

From the smallest of small town gyms to the world stage of the Olympics, gymnastics are one of America's most popular sports. And there's a constant supply of youngsters eager to join in the fun.

The floor exercises require strength and flexibility.

Gymnastics are more than just an exciting sport to watch. Gymnastics develop muscle strength, balance, and overall physical flexibility. What's more, all of these add up to give the young gymnast a great sense of self esteem and confidence.

Gymnastics are wonderful for the body and mind. They also provide a possible doorway to worldwide adventure. With competitions all over the world, the chance is always there to meet kids from other countries, to see other lifestyles, and to experience other **cultures**.

Girls compete in four events: the uneven parallel bars, floor, balance beam, and vault. Boys compete in six events: **vault**, **horizontal** bar, floor, rings, pommel horse, and **parallel** bars.

Even if you're performing cartwheels in a parade, you're doing gymnastics.

IN THE BEGINNING

There is evidence that gymnastics are more than 3,000 years old. Based on examples of artwork, many historians believe gymnastics began in ancient Egypt and grew during the times of the Greek and Roman empires.

Gymnastics have expanded to include Rhythmic Gymnastics, using props like balls, hoops, scarves, and ropes; and Sports Acrobatics, which features balancing stunts and tumbling.

This gymnast also has the ability to demonstrate the grace and beauty of a dancer.

THE BASICS

Before starting any training session, it's very important to warm up and stretch. Gymnasts need muscle strength as well as **stamina** and endurance, so it's important to take conditioning seriously, to eat a balanced diet, and to get plenty of sleep each night.

It's always a good idea to work with a partner who can serve as a spotter. This is someone who will make sure you don't get injured while you're learning new **maneuvers**.

One basic item in every gymnast's gear bag is hand protection, which is used on the uneven, high, and parallel bars.

The start of any gymnastic career begins with a few basic skills that will focus on building strength and balance. They include the Forward Roll (a somersault, basically), the Backward Roll, the Headstand, the Handstand, the Cartwheel, and a variety of graceful jumps.

When you're learning to do a handstand, it's a good idea to use a spotter and also to position yourself a foot or so away from a wall. This will help keep you from flopping over backward. Once you establish your balance, bring your feet away from the wall and hold the handstand as long as you can.

Once you've mastered a handstand on the floor, you can do it anywhere!

With both the forward and backward rolls, it's important to tuck your chin to your chest to protect yourself from a neck injury. You will use your hands and arms to support most of your weight in both of these rolls, as well as to gain balance as you rotate.

This gymnast is in a tuck position as she completes a flip during her floor exercise.

FLOOR SKILLS

There is a lot of running, jumping, and tumbling in both boys' and girls' gymnastics. Most of it takes place in the floor exercises. There are also some challenging flips and strength positions to master with practice and **repetition**.

The Handspring—also called a round-off—is a very common gymnastic move. Start by jumping forward onto your hands. Then whip your torso and legs quickly over the top. Finish by springing off your hands and landing gracefully on both feet.

It takes a tremendous amount of balance and strength to hold a basic acrobatic position.

VAULTING

Both girls and boys participate in the vault. This event begins by sprinting up the runway. After launching from the spring box, do a handspring off the horse. Finish with a mid-air tumbling trick and then land gracefully and in complete control.

The vaulting event includes three steps: the runway, the box (a springboard at the end of the runway), and the vaulting horse, a 64-inch- (163 cm-) long padded bolster to vault over.

Here's the vault—the big picture from end to end.

ACROMAT

Vaulting combines explosive speed (the sprint to the box), strength (planting and launching off the vaulting horse itself), and **agility** (the aerial stunt). Vaulters perform flips, turns, and somersaults while airborne, which makes landing upright and on two feet that much harder.

Vaulters have to run at top speed when they want to hit the box that will send them airborne.

There are some differences between boys' and girls' vaulting. Girls (and women) vault across the width of the horse and have two chances to make their vault. Boys (and men) vault across the length of the horse and receive only one attempt to complete their vault successfully.

The "horse" is lightly padded for safety. It is usually covered in some kind of non-skid material like **suede**, so vaulters won't lose grip at high speeds.

A vaulter hits the horse and transfers his weight into the forward airborne tumbling trick.

THE BALANCE BEAM

The Balance Beam **apparatus** is used only by girls and can be nerve-wracking to watch. It's hard enough to complete jumps, leaps, somersaults, back flips, and cartwheels on the floor. Imagine doing it on a 4-inch- (10-cm-) wide beam 4 feet (1.2 m) above the floor.

As if it isn't hard enough to leap into the air and do a perfect split, imagine having to land on a narrow strip of wood!

The balance beam itself is up to 16 feet (4.9 m) long. Gymnasts in this event will perform a series of moves that demonstrate strength, agility, gracefulness, and, of course, balance. Once the routine is finished, the gymnast must perform a tricky dismount as well.

The best way to learn the balance beam is to use a 4-inch- (10-cm-) wide foam strip on the floor. The single most important key to a successful balance beam gymnast is gaining confidence.

It takes a lot of courage to do back flips on a beam that is just 4 inches (10 cm) wide.

THE BARS

Boys and girls alike compete on equipment featuring bars. Girls use the uneven parallel bars (also called the asymmetrical bars). Boys, however, use the parallel bars and the horizontal (or high) bar. Both of these events require a lot of strength and flexibility.

The uneven parallel bars are part of the girls' menu of events.

Routines performed by girls on the uneven parallel bars have some basic requirements. Athletes must include swings, circles, and specific handstand positions in which they come to a complete stop. Girls must also release from one bar to the other and complete aerial moves.

The horizontal bar has many of the same **mandatory** elements as the girls' uneven bars. The bar itself measures about 8 feet (2.4 m) long and is usually set about 8 feet (2.4 m) off the ground. It flexes and bends, adding to the gymnast's motion as he swings, releases, and executes airborne stunts.

The horizontal bar is a high-action event with swinging and airborne tumbling.

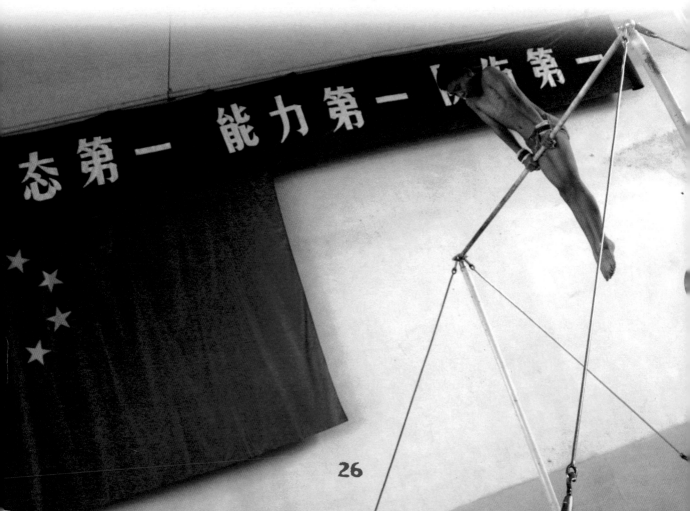

态第一　能力第一

The parallel bars are set at equal height (unlike the girls' uneven parallel bars). Competitors must travel above, between, and beneath the bars using only their hands and arms. Flips, turns, handstands, and release-and-catch moves are all fundamental elements of this exciting event.

Bart Conner, one of America's greatest gymnasts, won an olympic gold medal in the parallel bars at the 1984 summer games in Los Angeles.

There is a quiet grace to the parallel bars, one of the boys' events.

ADVANCED APPARATUS

The rings are among the hardest events in all of gymnastics. This is a pure power event. Athletes execute a series of swinging moves leading to postures in which they hold absolutely still. Control and concentration are extremely important on the rings.

基本 第一

The hanging rings are one of the most difficult of all gymnastic events.

The pommel horse is another event requiring great strength and agility. Athletes support their weight on two pommels (handles) while completing a series of skill moves. To score high marks, they must stay above the horse. Like all gymnastic events, it takes a lot of practice to get it right, but the end result is really satisfying.

The pommel horse is one of the events for men only.

GLOSSARY

agility (uh JIL ut ee) — the ability to move in a quick, easy, graceful fashion

apparatus (AP uh RAT us) — a machine or series of machines designed for a special purpose

cultures (KUL churz) — the patterns and beliefs of a society

horizontal (hor ih ZON tal) — parallel to the horizon (the ground)

maneuvers (mah NOO verz) — physical movements requiring skill or dexterity

mandatory (MAN duh tor ee) — something required by rules or law

parallel (PAHR uh lel) — being an equal distant apart at every point

repetition (REP eh TISH un) — the act of repeating

stamina (STAM uh nuh) — the physical strength to withstand fatigue

suede (SWAYD) — leather with a soft surface

vault (VAWLT) — to jump or leap over

Further Reading

Goeller, Karen M. *Most Frequently Asked Questions About Gymnastics.* Booklocker.com, 2003

Herran, Joe & Thomas, Ron. *Gymnastics.* Chelsea House Publishers, 2003

Morley, Christine. *The Best Book of Gymnastics.* Houghton Mifflin Company, 2003

Porter, David. *Winning Gymnastics for Girls.* Facts on File, 2004

Websites to Visit

Gymnastics Resources @ utyx.com/gymnastics/

International Gymnastics Hall of Fame @ www.ighof.com/

USA Gymnastics @ www.usa-gymnastics.org/

Index

About the Author

Morgan Hughes is the author of more than 50 books on hockey, track and field, bicycling, and many other subjects. He lives in Connecticut with his wife, daughter, and son.